I Can Read Now!

This book belongs to:

_____

My school is:

_____

I am _____ years old.

I Can Read Now!

Easy Sight Words for Developing Young Readers

David Fernstedt

Illustrated by Michael Menard

r
FOR
YOUNG
READERS

Visit our website at www.skyhorsepublishing.com.

10 9 8 7 6 5 4 3

Library of Congress Cataloging-in-Publication Data is available on file.

Cover illustration by Michael Menard

ISBN: 978-1-63158-360-5
Ebook ISBN: 978-1-63158-361-2

Printed in China

A Note to Parents and Educators

I created the concept (*sentence pyramids*) that you will find within these pages as a tool to help my own children learn to read using sight words. We had tried flash cards with only very little success, and found that the *sentence pyramid* was a much more effective method to teach sight word reading. The sight words with in this book are the one hundred fifty most commonly used words in the English language as identified by a popular spelling program. When looking for sight words for this book, I found that many schools utilize this list of common words as their sight word list using fifty to one hundred fifty of these words. As a result, these were the words that I chose. Along with those one hundred fifty common words, I added everyday words such as car, truck, cat, dog, as well as colors and numbers. The sentences are in a context that children will relate to, and teach through the use of sight, sound, color, and repetition. I think that you will find that children love this book. The *sentence pyramid* allows them to focus on one word at a time, and in seconds they are able to read their first sentence. Through the use of repetition, this method builds a lot of confidence in the child. The child will also love the illustrations. Each illustration was carefully designed to bring the sentences to life, while instilling values such as caring, sharing, family togetherness, respect, responsibility, sportsmanship, team work, friendship, cooperation, choice and consequences. Reading should be enjoyable for the child. This book makes reading fun. It also serves as a great first step to reading. I hope that you find this book to be both enjoyable and an effective tool to teach reading.

Thank you,
David Fernstedt

Introduction

This book will help you, help your child begin to read. This book is intended as a first step prior to learning *phonics*. Your child needs to know the alphabet prior to beginning this book. Sit down with your child, say the red word in each line, one line at a time. Have your child repeat that word on the next line, then you say the next word (again in red). Continue this pattern until your child can read the last sentence of the page by him/her self. Then repeat the page, until your child can read the page by him/her self. Your child should be able to read the words on each page quickly. You have now helped your child take his/her first steps towards becoming a *great* reader.

Good luck!
David Fernstedt

Word List

a	each	kids	ran	very
about	even	know	read	
after	eyes		red	was
all		lap	ride	water
am	far	like	roll	way
an	fast	likes	run	we
and	favorite	little		were
apple	find	long	said	what
apples	first		sat	when
are	five	made	say	where
as	for	make	school	which
at	found	many	see	white
	from	may	she	who
back		me	shop	why
ball	gave	moon	sit	will
be	get	more	sky	with
bee	girl	most	snack	words
been	go	my	so	would
before	going		some	
best	got	night	sun	yellow
big	grass	no		yes
bigger	green	not	tall	you
black		now	taller	your
blue	had		than	
book	hard	of	that	zoo
boy	has	on	the	
bright	have	one	their	
brown	he	only	them	
but	her	open	then	
by	hers	or	there	
	hill	orange	these	
call	him	other	they	
called	his	our	thought	
can	how	out	this	
car		over	time	
cat	I		to	
come	if	paint	today	
comes	in	people	too	
could	into	pet	toys	
	is	pies	truck	
desk	it	play	two	
did	its	pop		
do			up	
dog	jump		us	
dogs	just		use	
down				

Color me!

I
I can
I can see
I can see the
I can see the dog.
I can see the dog.

Can

Can you

Can you see

Can you see the

Can you see the dog?

Can you see the dog?

Can
Can you
Can you see
Can you see the
Can you see the cat?
Can you see the cat?

The
The cat
The cat is
The cat is in
The cat is in the
The cat is in the tree
The cat is in the tree by
The cat is in the tree by the
The cat is in the tree by the box.
The cat is in the tree by the box.

Your
Your dog
Your dog is
Your dog is a
Your dog is a big
Your dog is a big dog.
Your dog is a big dog.

My
My dog
My dog is
My dog is big
My dog is big too.
My dog is big too.

Can
Can you
Can you see
Can you see the
Can you see the boy
Can you see the boy play
Can you see the boy play with
Can you see the boy play with the
Can you see the boy play with the dog?
Can you see the boy play with the dog?

He
He got
He got a
He got a new
He got a new red
He got a new red ball
He got a new red ball from
He got a new red ball from his
He got a new red ball from his dad.
He got a new red ball from his dad.

Color Me!

I
I can
I can run,
I can run, can
I can run, can you?
I can run, can you?

9.

Yes!
Yes! I
Yes! I can
Yes! I can run
Yes! I can run too.
Yes! I can run too.

The
The girl
The girl can
The girl can jump.
The girl can jump.

I
I can
I can jump
I can jump too!
I can jump too! Can
I can jump too! Can you?
I can jump too! Can you?

My
My dog
My dog can
My dog can sit.
My dog can sit.

He
He can
He can roll
He can roll over
He can roll over too!
He can roll over too!

We
We each
We each have
We each have a
We each have a pet.
We each have a pet.

Each
Each of
Each of us
Each of us has
Each of us has a
Each of us has a pet.
Each of us has a pet.

I
I like
I like this
I like this dog
I like this dog and
I like this dog and she
I like this dog and she likes
I like this dog and she likes that
I like this dog and she likes that one.
I like this dog and she likes that one.

Which
Which of
Which of the
Which of the dogs
Which of the dogs do
Which of the dogs do you
Which of the dogs do you like?
Which of the dogs do you like?

I

I like

I like the

I like the black

I like the black dog.

I like the black dog. She

I like the black dog. She likes

I like the black dog. She likes the

I like the black dog. She likes the brown

I like the black dog. She likes the brown one.

I like the black dog. She likes the brown one.

Which
Which one
Which one do
Which one do you
Which one do you like
Which one do you like best?
Which one do you like best?

My
My cat
My cat has
My cat has two
My cat has two green
My cat has two green eyes.
My cat has two green eyes.

His
His dog
His dog has
His dog has two
His dog has two brown
His dog has two brown eyes.
His dog has two brown eyes.

Do
Do you
Do you see
Do you see the
Do you see the blue
Do you see the blue car?
Do you see the blue car?

Yes,
Yes, I
Yes, I see
Yes, I see the
Yes, I see the blue
Yes, I see the blue car.
Yes, I see the blue car.

Do
Do you
Do you see
Do you see the
Do you see the black
Do you see the black and
Do you see the black and yellow
Do you see the black and yellow bee?
Do you see the black and yellow bee?

Yes
Yes I
Yes I see
Yes I see the
Yes I see the black
Yes I see the black and
Yes I see the black and yellow
Yes I see the black and yellow bee.
Yes I see the black and yellow bee.

Do
Do you
Do you see
Do you see the
Do you see the big
Do you see the big red
Do you see the big red ball?
Do you see the big red ball?

I
I can
I can see
I can see the
I can see the big
I can see the big red
I can see the big red ball.
I can see the big red ball. Can
I can see the big red ball. Can you?
I can see the big red ball. Can you?

I
I can
I can get
I can get the
I can get the red
I can get the red ball
I can get the red ball but
I can get the red ball but not
I can get the red ball but not the
I can get the red ball but not the yellow
I can get the red ball but not the yellow one.
I can get the red ball but not the yellow one.

She
She can
She can not
She can not get
She can not get the
She can not get the yellow
She can not get the yellow ball.
She can not get the yellow ball.

The
The sky
The sky is
The sky is blue,
The sky is blue, and
The sky is blue, and the
The sky is blue, and the grass
The sky is blue, and the grass is
The sky is blue, and the grass is green.
The sky is blue, and the grass is green.

31.

The
The sun
The sun is
The sun is yellow,
The sun is yellow, and
The sun is yellow, and the
The sun is yellow, and the moon
The sun is yellow, and the moon is
The sun is yellow, and the moon is white.
The sun is yellow, and the moon is white.

The
The sun
The sun is
The sun is big
The sun is big and
The sun is big and bright.
The sun is big and bright.

The
The moon
The moon comes
The moon comes out
The moon comes out at
The moon comes out at night.
The moon comes out at night.

A
A big
A big brown
A big brown dog
A big brown dog ran
A big brown dog ran down
A big brown dog ran down the
A big brown dog ran down the hill.
A big brown dog ran down the hill.

The
The big
The big brown
The big brown dog
The big brown dog ran
The big brown dog ran fast.
The big brown dog ran fast.

I

I like

I like my

I like my little

I like my little orange

I like my little orange truck.

I like my little orange truck.

I
I like
I like my
I like my yellow
I like my yellow truck
I like my yellow truck too.
I like my yellow truck too.

I
I am
I am going
I am going to
I am going to go
I am going to go to
I am going to go to the
I am going to go to the zoo
I am going to go to the zoo today.
I am going to go to the zoo today.

We
We will
We will go
We will go to
We will go to the
We will go to the zoo
We will go to the zoo today.
We will go to the zoo today.

Can

Can you

Can you come

Can you come to

Can you come to the

Can you come to the zoo

Can you come to the zoo with

Can you come to the zoo with us?

Can you come to the zoo with us?

Yes,
Yes, I
Yes, I can
Yes, I can come
Yes, I can come to
Yes, I can come to the
Yes, I can come to the zoo
Yes, I can come to the zoo with
Yes, I can come to the zoo with you.
Yes, I can come to the zoo with you.

Can
Can you
Can you read
Can you read this
Can you read this book?
Can you read this book?

Yes,
Yes, I
Yes, I can
Yes, I can read
Yes, I can read this
Yes, I can read this book.
Yes, I can read this book.

I
I can
I can read
I can read now!
I can read now!

He
He can
He can read
He can read that
He can read that book.
He can read that book.

This
This book
This book is
This book is his
This book is his and
This book is his and that
This book is his and that book
This book is his and that book is
This book is his and that book is hers.
This book is his and that book is hers.

He
He is
He is a
He is a boy,
He is a boy, and
He is a boy, and she
He is a boy, and she is
He is a boy, and she is a
He is a boy, and she is a girl.
He is a boy, and she is a girl.

He
He gave
He gave her
He gave her an
He gave her an apple.
He gave her an apple.

She
She gave
She gave him
She gave him one
She gave him one too.
She gave him one too.

We
We can
We can each
We can each have
We can each have an
We can each have an apple.
We can each have an apple.

If
If we
If we each
If we each have
If we each have two
If we each have two apples
If we each have two apples then
If we each have two apples then we
If we each have two apples then we will
If we each have two apples then we will be
If we each have two apples then we will be even.
If we each have two apples then we will be even.

color me!

Who

Who would

Who would like

Who would like an

Who would like an apple?

Who would like an apple?

These
These are
These are the
These are the very
These are the very best
These are the very best apples!
These are the very best apples!

She
She gave
She gave him
She gave him some
She gave him some of
She gave him some of her
She gave him some of her toys.
She gave him some of her toys.

He
He gave
He gave her
He gave her some
He gave her some of
He gave her some of his
He gave her some of his toys
He gave her some of his toys too!
He gave her some of his toys too!

They
They have
They have more
They have more kids
They have more kids than
They have more kids than we
They have more kids than we do.
They have more kids than we do.

We
We have
We have two
We have two kids
We have two kids but
We have two kids but they
We have two kids but they have
We have two kids but they have four.
We have two kids but they have four.

Which
Which do
Which do you
Which do you like?
Which do you like? This
Which do you like? This or
Which do you like? This or that?
Which do you like? This or that?

59.

I
I will
I will have
I will have this
I will have this and
I will have this and you
I will have this and you may
I will have this and you may have
I will have this and you may have that.
I will have this and you may have that.

Color Me!

I
I like
I like this
I like this but
I like this but not
I like this but not that.
I like this but not that.

61.

This
This is
This is as
This is as good
This is as good as
This is as good as that.
This is as good as that.

Where
Where have
Where have you
Where have you been?
Where have you been?

I
I have
I have been
I have been playing
I have been playing at
I have been playing at the
I have been playing at the park.
I have been playing at the park.

What
What did
What did you
What did you put
What did you put on
What did you put on my
What did you put on my desk?
What did you put on my desk?

I

I sat

I sat my

I sat my open

I sat my open can

I sat my open can of

I sat my open can of pop

I sat my open can of pop up

I sat my open can of pop up there.

I sat my open can of pop up there.

What
What about
What about me?
What about me?

Why
Why was
Why was that
Why was that so
Why was that so hard
Why was that so hard to
Why was that so hard to say?
Why was that so hard to say?

Color me!

Their
Their car
Their car is
Their car is bigger
Their car is bigger than
Their car is bigger than our
Their car is bigger than our car.
Their car is bigger than our car.

69.

This
This one
This one is
This one is bigger
This one is bigger than
This one is bigger than that
This one is bigger than that one.
This one is bigger than that one.

How
How far
How far is
How far is it
How far is it from
How far is it from here
How far is it from here to
How far is it from here to there?
How far is it from here to there?

We
We should
We should be
We should be there
We should be there by
We should be there by now.
We should be there by now.

We
We were
We were at
We were at the
We were at the zoo
We were at the zoo today.
We were at the zoo today.

They
They have
They have been
They have been at
They have been at the
They have been at the zoo
They have been at the zoo too.
They have been at the zoo too.

About
About how
About how many
About how many pies
About how many pies did
About how many pies did she
About how many pies did she make?
About how many pies did she make?

She
She just
She just made
She just made five
She just made five pies.
She just made five pies.

He
He is
He is about
He is about as
He is about as tall
He is about as tall as
He is about as tall as her.
He is about as tall as her.

Is
Is she
Is she taller
Is she taller than
Is she taller than him?
Is she taller than him?

He
He is
He is very
He is very tall.
He is very tall.

He
He is
He is taller
He is taller than
He is taller than most
He is taller than most people.
He is taller than most people.

Where
Where will
Where will you
Where will you be
Where will you be after
Where will you be after school?
Where will you be after school?

We
We will
We will be
We will be at
We will be at the
We will be at the lake
We will be at the lake after
We will be at the lake after school.
We will be at the lake after school.

Their
Their dog
Their dog is
Their dog is a
Their dog is a little
Their dog is a little dog.
Their dog is a little dog.

Our
Our dog
Our dog is
Our dog is a
Our dog is a big
Our dog is a big dog.
Our dog is a big dog.

Where
Where did
Where did you
Where did you find
Where did you find that
Where did you find that toy?
Where did you find that toy?

I
I found
I found it
I found it in
I found it in the
I found it in the water.
I found it in the water.

I
I need
I need to
I need to know
I need to know how
I need to know how long
I need to know how long you
I need to know how long you will
I need to know how long you will be
I need to know how long you will be there.
I need to know how long you will be there.

I
I may
I may be
I may be there
I may be there a
I may be there a very
I may be there a very long
I may be there a very long time.
I may be there a very long time.

When
When will
When will we
When will we be
When will we be there?
When will we be there?

What
What time
What time will
What time will you
What time will you get
What time will you get here?
What time will you get here?

Before
Before you
Before you come
Before you come over,
Before you come over, could
Before you come over, could you
Before you come over, could you call
Before you come over, could you call first?
Before you come over, could you call first?

She
She called
She called before
She called before she
She called before she came
She called before she came over.
She called before she came over.

They
They each
They each had
They each had an
They each had an apple
They each had an apple as
They each had an apple as a
They each had an apple as a snack.
They each had an apple as a snack.

They
They thought
They thought all
They thought all of
They thought all of the
They thought all of the apples
They thought all of the apples were
They thought all of the apples were for
They thought all of the apples were for them.
They thought all of the apples were for them.

He
He said
He said it's
He said it's the
He said it's the only
He said it's the only way
He said it's the only way up
He said it's the only way up the
He said it's the only way up the hill.
He said it's the only way up the hill.

She
She said
She said that
She said that there
She said that there is
She said that there is no
She said that there is no other
She said that there is no other way
She said that there is no other way up
She said that there is no other way up the
She said that there is no other way up the hill.
She said that there is no other way up the hill.

Use
Use the
Use the green
Use the green paint
Use the green paint for
Use the green paint for the
Use the green paint for the grass.
Use the green paint for the grass.

Use
Use the
Use the blue
Use the blue paint
Use the blue paint for
Use the blue paint for the
Use the blue paint for the sky.
Use the blue paint for the sky.

Which
Which dog
Which dog was
Which dog was your
Which dog was your favorite?
Which dog was your favorite?

99.

The

The brown

The brown dog

The brown dog or

The brown dog or the

The brown dog or the yellow

The brown dog or the yellow dog?

The brown dog or the yellow dog?

The
The dog
The dog is
The dog is so
The dog is so big,
The dog is so big, I
The dog is so big, I can
The dog is so big, I can ride
The dog is so big, I can ride on
The dog is so big, I can ride on his
The dog is so big, I can ride on his back.
The dog is so big, I can ride on his back.

He
He is
He is too
He is too big
He is too big to
He is too big to sit
He is too big to sit on
He is too big to sit on my
He is too big to sit on my lap.
He is too big to sit on my lap.